T0014711

# NOTHING COULD
# STOP HER

# NOTHING COULD STOP HER

## STOP HER

The Courageous
Life of Ruth
Gruber

Rona Arato

Illustrated by Isabel Muñoz

**KAR-BEN**
PUBLISHING

Thanks to the Ontario Arts Council and
PJ Our Way for their generous support.
—R. A.

Text copyright © 2023 by Rona Arato
Illustrations copyright © 2023 by Lerner Publishing Group, Inc.

All rights reserved. International copyright secured. No part of this book may be reproduced, stored in a retrieval system, or transmitted in any form or by any means—electronic, mechanical, photocopying, recording, or otherwise—without the prior written permission of Lerner Publishing Group, Inc., except for the inclusion of brief quotations in an acknowledged review.

KAR-BEN PUBLISHING®
An imprint of Lerner Publishing Group, Inc.
241 First Avenue North
Minneapolis, MN 55401 USA

Website address: www.karben.com

Illustrations by Isabel Muñoz.

Photos: Courtesy Everett Collection, p. 106; United States Holocaust Memorial Museum, courtesy of Marion Michel Oliner, p. 107.

Main body text set in Adobe Garamond Pro. Typeface provided by Adobe Systems.

**Library of Congress Cataloging-in-Publication Data**

Names: Arato, Rona, author.
Title: Nothing could stop her : the courageous life of Ruth Gruber / Rona Arato
Description: Minneapolis : Kar-Ben Publishing, [2023] | Includes bibliographical references. | Audience: Ages 8–12. | Audience: Grades 4–6. | Summary: "Ruth Gruber, born in to a Jewish American family in 1911, was drawn to adventure and driven to fight injustice throughout her eventful seven-decade career as a journalist" —Provided by publisher.
Identifiers: LCCN 2022008662 (print) | LCCN 2022008663 (ebook) | ISBN 9781728445618 (library binding) | ISBN 9781728445625 (paperback) | ISBN 9781728481166 (ebook)
Subjects: LCSH: Gruber, Ruth, 1911–2016—Juvenile literature. | Women journalists—United States—Biography—Juvenile literature. | Foreign correspondents—United States—Biography—Juvenile literature. | Jewish women—United States—Biography—Juvenile literature.
Classification: LCC PN4874.G78 A78 2023  (print) | LCC PN4874.G78  (ebook) | DDC 070.4332092—dc23/eng20220627

LC record available at https://lccn.loc.gov/2022008662
LC ebook record available at https://lccn.loc.gov/2022008663

Manufactured in the United States of America
1-50254-49871-7/8/2022

# CONTENTS

I had two tools to fight injustice—words
and images, my typewriter and my camera.
I just felt that I had to fight evil, and I've felt
like that since I was twenty years old.
And I've never been an observer. I have
to live a story to write it.

—*Ruth Gruber*

### Chapter 1

# Brooklyn

Ruth Gruber was born in 1911 in what she called a shtetl, a village—the Williamsburg neighborhood of Brooklyn, New York. Her parents, David and Gussie, were from Russia. Ruth was the fourth of their five children. She had two older brothers, Bob and Harry, and an older sister, Betty. Her youngest brother, Irving, was born in 1916, when Ruth was five and a half years old. The family lived in a small apartment above the liquor store that her father owned.

Ruth was a curious child who wanted to learn as much as possible about everything she saw and heard. She would sit on the curb watching tired horses pull wagons filled with fruit and vegetables. She'd listen to the calls of street peddlers. Every day, a tall man carried blocks of ice in huge iron claws up the stairs for the icebox in the Grubers' apartment. On his way down, he would give little Ruth a piece of ice, which she sucked as she watched the people on Moore Street go about their business.

\*\*\*

Because everyone she knew was Jewish, Ruth thought the whole world was Jewish. Moore Street smelled of briny pickles in big barrels, roasted sweet potatoes, and candy apples. People greeted each other in Yiddish.

Ruth loved Fridays, when the house smelled of freshly baked challah and almond cookies. At dusk, her mother lit the Shabbos candles and the family gathered around the dinner table. On Saturdays, the street was quiet—no horses or peddlers. Most stores

# Yiddish

Yiddish is the language of Ashkenazi (Eastern and Central European) Jews. It is written in the Hebrew alphabet and uses some Hebrew words. But it is also closely related to German. It originated in Europe, in the area that today is Germany, around the tenth century. Eventually, it became the main language of Jews living in Poland, Russia, and many other European countries. About 11 million people spoke the language before the Holocaust wiped out large populations of Yiddish speakers in the 1930s and 1940s. The language lives on, though, with about 600,000 Yiddish speakers worldwide. There are Yiddish theater companies, Yiddish musical groups, and even board games in Yiddish.

were closed, but Ruth's parents kept theirs open. They only closed their store for certain important Jewish holidays: Rosh Hashanah, Yom Kippur, and the first day of Passover. Every Saturday, Ruth's grandfather, Zayda Gruber, would take her to shul—synagogue. She'd sit with him downstairs, because although men and women sat separately, young girls could sit with the men. Ruth loved chanting the Hebrew prayers, even though she didn't understand the language. In those days, only boys attended Hebrew school.

After shul, her mother served a lunch of gefilte fish, chicken soup, and boiled chicken. Then Ruth and her sister Betty, who was two years older, would walk six blocks to visit their mother's parents. Their grandmother, Baba Rockower, fed them pastries, talked about her life in Russia, and read them articles from the Yiddish newspaper.

On the Jewish holidays when the store was closed, the whole family went to shul. On these days, Ruth and Betty sat upstairs with their mother and the other women, while their father and brothers were downstairs with the men. Ruth wished she could be with the men, like she was on Saturdays.

Ruth adored her father. David Gruber was six feet tall with a red mustache, gray-green eyes, and a soft voice that he never raised. Ruth's mother, Gussie, ruled the family. She had never finished school but was smart and taught her children the value of hard work.

Ruth's first lessons in helping others came from her father. Once a month, he sent money to relatives in Poland and Russia. And every spring, he asked his children for the clothes they weren't wearing so he could send them to Europe. If Ruth didn't want to part with a dress or coat, he would say, "Send it. They need it more than you."

Ruth's world opened up when she entered public school. Her first-grade teacher was a young Black woman who taught a class of Jewish, Irish, Polish, and Black girls.

## *Coney Island Adventures*

In the summers, Gussie would pack a picnic basket, gather her five children and assorted neighborhood kids, and take them on the trolley to the beach at Coney Island. There, she would spread a blanket and rest while the children splashed in the surf. Ruth loved those days at the ocean and loved her mother for giving them to her.

One day, Ruth's teacher knocked on the door of the Grubers' apartment. Ruth hid behind the bedroom door as her mother and the teacher spoke.

"Did she do something wrong?" Mrs. Gruber asked.

"No, no. I just wanted to tell you to take good care of her. She loves books so much. I'm sure that someday she's going to be a writer." Ruth never forgot those words.

\*\*\*

In 1920, the United States government made drinking or selling liquor illegal. Mr. Gruber closed his liquor store and began working in real estate. Meanwhile, the children were getting too big for the small house. Irving was five, Ruth was eleven, Betty was thirteen, and Bob and Harry were growing into young men. In 1921, the Grubers bought a house on Bushwick Avenue. It was only a mile away from Moore Street, but to Ruth it was a new world.

## Historic Tensions

Poland was sandwiched between two powerful neighbors, Russia to the east and Germany to the west. Both these countries invaded and controlled parts of Poland in the 1700s and 1800s. After World War I, Poland regained its independence. But many Poles remained suspicious of Germans and Russians. And many Protestant Germans distrusted Catholic and Jewish Poles.

Without realizing it, the family had moved into a German neighborhood. On spring and summer days, Ruth's brothers played softball in the street with the neighborhood boys. Ruth and Betty became friends with the boys' sisters. All the shopkeepers were German, including the man who ran the candy store where the family bought ice cream and Ruth's favorite dessert, charlotte russe—sponge cake topped with whipped cream. Everyone got along. But meanwhile, in Germany, a man named Adolf Hitler was telling crowds of cheering people that Jews were evil and that his goal was to destroy all the Jews in the world.

Chapter 2

# New Horizons

R uth was an extraordinary student. In those days, students
who excelled were often moved to higher grades. Ruth
skipped three grades in elementary school and was only twelve
when she entered high school.

As much as Ruth loved her Brooklyn neighborhood, she was
ready to expand her world. She wrote poems about her longing to
escape. Manhattan, with its tall buildings and mix of cultures, was
across the East River from Brooklyn. In 1926, at the age of fifteen,
Ruth graduated from high school and was admitted to New York
University, where she planned to major in German. At last, she
could explore the world beyond Brooklyn.

Each morning on her way to the university, Ruth took the
train to its last stop and then walked to the Williamsburg Bridge.
There, she paused to stare at the reflections of Manhattan
buildings mirrored upside down in the water. She wrote poems in
her head: "The soaring stone buildings reflected themselves in the
shimmering water, like two magical, identical cities, one real, the
other upside down."

From the bridge, Ruth walked through the crowded streets of

Manhattan's Lower East Side. She passed pushcarts where vendors sold fruits and vegetables, used clothing, and household tools. She stopped at her favorite secondhand bookstore and bought old books that she carried like hidden treasures. At Washington Square Park, she paused to look across the street at the gray glass-and-brick university building where she hoped her dreams would come true.

Ruth's English professor had her students write essays about themselves. She liked Ruth's essays and offered to submit them to the *Atlantic Monthly*, a prestigious literary magazine. Ruth was thrilled. When her stories were rejected, her professor told her not to be discouraged. "Go on writing," she said, adding that every writer could cover a room with rejection slips.

Ruth's German professor was a different matter. On the first day of class, he told his students to forget their Yiddish because it could spoil their German.

Forget Yiddish? Yiddish was the thread that tied Ruth to her parents, her grandparents, and the Jewish community. And she did not intend to let it stop her from becoming fluent in German.

\*\*\*

Now that she had broken free of Brooklyn, Ruth longed to keep exploring. Her German professor told her about a summer program at Mount Holyoke College in Massachusetts. Ruth was thrilled. This could be her chance to escape, even if just for six weeks.

When she told her parents about the program, her mother wasn't pleased. "You're too young to go away from home," she said.

But Ruth was determined. And her older brother Harry backed her up. "It's a good idea to know a foreign language so well that you can speak it like a native," he said.

Her brother Bob drove Ruth to the school, and for the next six weeks, Ruth did everything in German. She read German poetry, sang German songs, and spoke to her fellow students in German. Since Gruber is a German name, everyone thought that Ruth came from a German family and that she was related to Franz Gruber, the composer who wrote the Christmas carol "Silent Night." No matter how much Ruth protested, explaining that her family was Jewish and from Russia, they chose to believe that she was descended from the composer.

*\*\*\**

Back home in Brooklyn after the summer program ended, Ruth began planning her next getaway. She wanted to be a writer but knew it was hard to earn money from writing. And to be independent, she needed to earn money!

She saw an ad for a typing job and applied. Her new boss was the president of an association of Hungarian immigrants and refugees. Ruth worked as his typist for the rest of the year, often editing his words herself. Although she didn't receive credit for her contributions, she was proud of the work. And with the money she'd saved from her paychecks, she could afford to leave Brooklyn. But how would she leave?

The next step after a bachelor's degree was a master's degree. Ruth wanted to continue studying German, and soon she found a chance to do it. Her German professor nominated her for a fellowship with the University of Wisconsin's German department. She won the fellowship, which covered her full tuition for the university's year-long master's program in German, plus some of her living expenses.

Ruth was elated. Her parents were so proud of her for winning the fellowship that they didn't object, even when she told them she would hitchhike to Wisconsin. Hitchhiking—getting rides from strangers—was considered a safe way to travel at the time. Ruth's father got her a collection of road maps. Ruth spread the maps on the dining room table and planned her journey across New York State, through Michigan and Illinois, to Madison, Wisconsin. She was going to discover America.

Her mother patted her cheek. "My daughter the explorer."

Ruth shipped her clothes and books to Wisconsin. She packed a toothbrush, a change of clothes, and her maps in a tote bag. On a sunny August morning, Ruth kissed her family goodbye. Then she walked to the highway and stuck out her thumb to catch a ride.

Cars and trucks raced by. No one slowed down. Ruth waved her hand. The air was thick with heat. Finally, a couple with two young children stopped and picked her up. Ruth was on her way.

***

In Madison, Ruth moved into a small room in the German House, a dorm on campus. At last, she was independent, studying subjects that she loved. But she missed her family, especially the Friday night dinners with her mother lighting candles and her father reciting the Kiddush, the blessing over the wine. And Ruth was encountering something she had never known in Brooklyn—antisemitism. The woman in charge of the German House made Ruth painfully aware that she was the only Jew living there. When Ruth asked the head of the German department to find different housing for her, he was furious.

"You New Yorkers," he fumed. "You're all the same. You're always outsiders. You may be the brightest, but you think you can make your own rules. You can't."

Ruth ran out of his office. She knew that by *New Yorkers*, he really meant Jews. What should she do? She worried that if she left the German House, the German department would punish her by refusing to grant her a master's degree. But she couldn't live under those conditions. She found a room with a Norwegian family and left the dorm that very day.

***

In April, Ruth was at her desk, working on her master's thesis, when her landlady knocked on her door. She handed Ruth a crisp white envelope. Ruth opened it to find a letter: *You have been selected for* *a one-year exchange fellowship to the University of Cologne. You will receive your tuition and $1,000 for your living expenses.*

Ruth could hardly believe her eyes. She had applied for the grant to attend the German university but hadn't expected to get it. She was so excited that she hitchhiked home so she could tell her parents in person.

Instead of welcoming the news, Ruth's parents were horrified. Her father spoke for both of them.

"Ruthie, you're so young, just nineteen. I read terrible stories in the papers. They say this Adolf Hitler could take over Germany. What if it happens while you're there? Who knows what they could do to you?"

Ruth understood her parents' concerns. She knew Hitler's messages of hate were serious. Still, she squared her shoulders and stood as tall as her five-foot, two-inch frame would allow. "Papa, you wouldn't be so upset [. . .] if it was Bob or Harry or Irving," she said. "It's because I'm a girl."

Her father looked pained. "Don't go, Ruthie. I'll give you anything you want. Only don't go."

Ruth knew he only wanted what he thought was best for her, but she had to follow her own path. "Papa, you left Russia when you knew it was the right thing for you to do—to go to America. This is the right thing for me, Papa, and it's the right time for me to go to Germany."

Her father looked away. "I see I can't stop you."

"I'm sorry," Ruth told him. "Nobody can stop me." She was ready for the next chapter in her life.

## *Adolf Hitler*

Adolf Hitler (1889–1945) was an Austrian-born German politician. He was the leader of the Nazi Party and dictator of Germany from 1933 to 1945. In his book, *Mein Kampf* (My Struggle), he wrote about his hatred for Jews and his plans to exterminate them.

\*\*\*

Ruth hitchhiked back to Madison, finished her thesis, and received her master's degree. She couldn't wait to leave Madison, though. Her brother Bob and her sister, Betty, picked her up and drove her back to New York so she could pack for her trip to Germany.

Ruth would sail to Germany on a steamship. Her whole family came to the dock to see her off. Ruth's excitement was mixed with sadness and guilt. She was setting off on a great adventure, but she was leaving her family behind. She had missed them when she was in Madison. Germany was so much farther away. What would her life be like there? The antisemitism she'd experienced in Wisconsin had horrified her. She suspected it would be worse in Germany and wondered how she would cope with it.

Ruth put her worries aside to enjoy the ocean voyage. She wandered around the ship talking to passengers, officers, and deck hands. She described her experience to her family in a letter.

The Americans want to talk [about] books and literature and the Germans [. . .] The ones who hate [Hitler] tell me he's a clown [. . .] They're sure the good [people] of Germany will never let him come to power. The ones who love him tell me he'll take over by 1932. My God, that's only next year! What a year this will be.

Chapter 3

# A Year in Germany

Ruth arrived in Cologne, Germany, in September 1931. The university had arranged for her to stay with a Jewish family. Frieda Herz was a small, friendly woman who reminded Ruth of her mother. Frieda's husband, Otto, a successful businessman, took on the role of Ruth's father. Their twenty-year-old daughter, Luisa, quickly became Ruth's best friend.

Ruth took classes in German and English literature. She often brought fellow students home to dinner. Sunday nights were her favorite: informal meals when they ate potato pancakes with applesauce and talked about literature and politics. One night, when her friend Nathan was visiting, the talk turned to Hitler and his followers. Nathan believed they were more dangerous than most people realized. Mr. Herz disagreed. He thought Hitler had no real political power.

But Nathan warned that Hitler was working to get bankers, publishers, and other businesses on his side. Once Hitler got elected to a leadership position in the German government, he would go after the Jews.

Ruth couldn't ignore Nathan's comments as easily as the

Herzes. How bad was the situation in Germany? Should she be worried? And would she have to abandon her studies and return to the United States? She decided to stay and see what happened next.

***

Ruth's decision to remain in Germany was strengthened when a professor at the university asked to see her. And this wasn't just any professor—Professor Schoffler was in charge of the English Language and Literature department. He thought Ruth should earn a PhD (doctor of philosophy) degree while she was in

# Nazism

The National Socialist German Workers' Party, or Nazi Party, formed around 1920. World War I (1914–1918) had left Germany defeated and in economic trouble. The country had lost a lot of land and had to pay other countries for the damage the war had caused. People didn't have jobs or money. The Nazi Party encouraged Christian Germans to blame minority groups, especially Jews, for the country's problems.

The Nazi Party grew into a mass movement that ruled Germany from 1933 to 1945 under the leadership of Adolf Hitler. Hitler and the Nazi Party played on people's fears and prejudices, pledging to make Germany strong again. Nazis believed in totalitarian rule, meaning one leader was the supreme authority to enforce Nazism's nationalistic, racist, and antisemitic policies.

Cologne. He suggested that she do original research on the English author Virginia Woolf.

Ruth was stunned. She was interested in Woolf's work, but she explained that her grant was only for one year.

Professor Schoffler smiled. "No one's ever gotten a PhD in one year," he said. "But let's try."

The professor had given Ruth a challenge she couldn't refuse. She scoured bookstores for every book Virginia Woolf had ever written. She decided to write about Woolf's determination to live life on her own terms—a determination that mirrored Ruth's feelings. After all, Ruth was not following the usual path for a young woman—to get married and have children. She was here in Germany, pursuing something that was supposed to be impossible: to get an advanced degree in one year.

*** 

One person Ruth didn't invite to the Herzes' home was her friend Johann, another PhD student. She wasn't sure why. Was it because Johann wasn't Jewish?

She and Johann enjoyed many long walks along the River Rhine, discussing German history and politics. Ruth asked him about the rising tide of antisemitism. Why were more and more students coming to the university in brown shirts, the Nazi Youth uniform? And what about the JEWS NOT WANTED signs in cafes and shops? What about the hate-filled headlines in the German newspapers?

Johann admitted Germany was going through a difficult time but assured her that the Nazis wouldn't last. Ruth wanted to believe him. Yet everything she saw and heard seemed to contradict his words.

*** 

In November 1931, Ruth joined a group of American students on a ski trip. During the train ride to the mountains, Ruth read *Mein Kampf*, the book that Hitler had written in 1924 to tell the world his plans for the Nazi Party.

As she read line after line of antisemitic rants blaming Jews for all of Germany's troubles, her anger mounted. She looked at her fellow passengers. Could that sweet-faced woman eating a ham sandwich agree with Hitler? How about the gray-haired man smoking a pipe or the blond-haired girl gazing out the window?

These thoughts stayed with her until she reached her destination—a quaint village with a charming ski lodge. She had never skied, but she was ready to give it a try. The mountain air was cold and crisp. The snow sparkled in the sunlight. For a while, Ruth could focus on trying—and failing—to stay upright on the slopes.

But that evening, her group was invited to a party in town. While people ate, drank, and sang German folk songs, a young man sitting next to Ruth turned to her. "I don't like Americans," he said. "They're loud and vulgar. But you're different."

Ruth was offended but tried to be polite. "I don't agree with you that all Americans are loud and vulgar."

"American Jews are the worst," he went on. "Hitler is right. We have to get rid of them before they take over the world."

Ruth jumped to her feet. "I am an American and a Jew, and I will not listen to such talk."

She stormed out of the restaurant.

Her group's American chaperone followed her. "You had no right to speak to that man the way you did. I want you to go back and apologize."

"Apologize! He insulted me," Ruth replied angrily. "Let him apologize to me!"

But she knew that wouldn't happen. And she knew no one else would stand up to him.

The fun of the ski trip was ruined for her. She decided to leave immediately.

\*\*\*

The next morning, Ruth took the train to visit Vienna, the capital of Austria. She knew one person there, Betty's friend Norman. He had moved there to attend medical school because American schools often rejected Jewish applicants. Ruth asked Norman to show her the university where he was studying.

"I'm not sure you'll like what I have to show you." Reluctantly, he took her to the chemistry lab where he did experiments. It looked as if there had been an earthquake or a bomb blast. Shattered glass beakers and torn-up notebook paper littered the floor.

"Nazis?" Ruth asked, horrified.

"Nazi students," Norman confirmed. "They must have come in the middle of the night. Just to this lab. They knew most of us were Jews." Norman's voice was full of sadness. "Months of work, all destroyed."

Ruth was furious. She'd known there were Nazi students in Cologne. But now she saw that the surge in violent antisemitism extended beyond Germany.

Ruth had a sinking feeling that Europe and its people were headed in a very dangerous direction.

Chapter 4

# A Historic Election

Ruth stood at the back of the crowded exhibition hall, her anger so thick she felt it would choke her. Out of grim curiosity, she had decided to attend a Nazi rally.

The hall was filled with people of all ages. Young men wearing brown shirts with swastika armbands stood tall, as if they owned the world. On the stage, in front of a banner with an enormous swastika, Adolf Hitler was whipping the crowd into a frenzy by screaming "Death to the Jews." Around her, people cheered.

When she couldn't stand it anymore, Ruth slipped outside. She breathed in gulps of air, as if to cleanse herself of Hitler's poisonous words. She walked to the river and stared down at the water. In New York, the water had soothed her. But here, nothing could wash away the nightmare she had just witnessed.

May 13, 1932, was Election Day for Germany's president. That night, Ruth sat in the Herzes' living room listening to the news on the radio. The election results came in: President Hindenburg's party had won 49.6 percent of the votes, slightly short of the 50 percent needed to be the ruling party. Hitler and the Nazi Party had come in second with 30.1 percent.

"Thirty percent of the German people want Hitler!" Ruth exclaimed. "It's sickening."

Since no party had gotten a majority of votes, a second election was held on April 10. This time, Hindenburg won 53 percent of the vote. Ruth rejoiced with the Herzes.

Their optimism didn't last long, though. In May, Hindenburg fired his anti-Nazi chancellor. The next election was scheduled for

July 31, when Germans would vote for members of the Reichstag, Germany's main governing body. Hitler's supporters plastered posters all over Cologne. They stood on street corners screaming insults about the other parties—and about Jews.

The mood in the Herz home became grim. Ruth felt the family's fear. On the night of July 31, they huddled around the radio. The announcer said that Hitler's party had won 230 of the Reichstag's 608 seats—more than any other party. Mr. Herz banged his fist on the table. "Awful. Awful. They were a nothing party in 1928. And now, in three years, look at them. The biggest party in Germany."

Ruth was worried for her Jewish friends. She asked the Herzes if they would consider leaving Germany for somewhere safer. But they replied that they were Germans, and this was their home. Ruth also knew it wasn't easy to get into other countries, especially the United States. Since 1924, the US government had placed

## Immigration Quotas

The Emergency Quota Act of 1924 limited the number of immigrants from certain countries and backgrounds who could enter the United States. There were strict quotas—or limits— for Jews, Italians, Greeks, and people from Eastern European countries such as Poland. This meant that most Jews hoping to escape Nazi persecution in the 1930s were barred from entering the United States.

strict quotas on Jews, Italians, Greeks, and people from Eastern European countries such as Poland who wanted to immigrate to the United States. Many white, Christian Americans distrusted immigrants from these backgrounds.

Ruth decided that when she went home, she would tell her fellow Americans about what was happening in Germany. She would try to convince people that US immigration rules needed to change so that more Jews could escape to safety. But first, she had to complete her fellowship.

For the rest of the year, Ruth concentrated on finishing her dissertation on Virginia Woolf. She was only twenty when she received her PhD.

\*\*\*

In August, Ruth left Germany to return home. Saying goodbye to the Herzes made her heart ache. They had become her German family. But she wasn't going to miss Germany.

Johann wanted her to stay. He told her that some of the changes in Germany were for the better. The Nazis, he said, were building the country's economy and giving Germans back their self-respect.

But at what cost? Ruth demanded.

Johann didn't answer, but Ruth saw her worst fears reflected in his eyes.

\*\*\*

On August 31, 1932, Ruth's ship, the *St. Louis*, sailed into New York Harbor, past Ellis Island, where her parents had landed as immigrants. A woman beside Ruth sobbed. "Dear God, to leave Germany and see this statue! Do you know what this means?"

Ruth put her arms around the woman. "I think maybe I do."

Ruth's parents were waiting for her on the dock, along with her fifteen-year-old brother Irving. As she walked down the gangplank, Ruth saw a group of reporters and photographers waiting at the bottom. Ruth thought there must be a movie star onboard.

"How does it feel to be the youngest PhD in the world?" called a reporter. A woman next to him pointed a camera at Ruth. Other reporters crowded around her.

Ruth felt overwhelmed. She pushed her way through the crowd and threw herself into the arms of her family. "Get me out of here!"

# *The St. Louis*

The ship that took Ruth home in 1932 would become famous a few years later. In 1939, it was carrying European Jews fleeing Nazism. The ship and its refugees were turned away by the governments of the United States, Canada, and Cuba. Eventually the ship was forced to return to Europe, where many of the passengers died in the Holocaust.

In the car, her mother said that the family's phone had been ringing for days. When they reached their house, Ruth saw reporters and photographers waiting outside. For the next several weeks, she was bombarded with requests for interviews. Ruth couldn't believe that she was a celebrity. But what she needed was a job.

In the United States, like most of the world, many people were out of work. Those who couldn't afford to buy food had to wait in long bread lines for meager rations. With jobs so scarce, Ruth wasn't sure how she was going to earn a living. But she remembered the words of her teacher: "She's going to be a writer." And that was what Ruth was determined to do.

***

Writing was easy for Ruth, but selling her work was not. Most reporters and newspaper editors were men, and women had to fight to be taken seriously in the business.

# *The Great Depression*

The Great Depression was a severe worldwide economic downturn that began with the 1929 stock market crash and lasted through the 1930s. Millions of people worldwide suffered joblessness, homelessness, and hunger. Hitler blamed the Jews for causing the depression and used its consequences to gather support for his Nazi policies.

She refused to be discouraged. She wrote an article about the vibrant, diverse Brooklyn neighborhoods where she'd grown up. She wrote about the kosher butchers, Polish delicatessens, pushcarts selling fruit and vegetables, and peddlers selling roasted chestnuts in the winter and ice cream in the summer. She painted word pictures of people dancing in the street during festivals and of laughing children splashing in the water from an open fire hydrant on steamy summer days. She sold the article to the *New York Times*. She then sold several other pieces to the *New York Herald Tribune*.

Ruth had launched her career as a writer.

Chapter 5

# Back to Europe

R uth's worst fears came true in 1933. Hitler was elected chancellor of Germany and began enacting anti-Jewish laws. Ruth worried about the Herzes and her other Jewish friends in Germany.

By now, Ruth was regularly writing stories for the *Herald Tribune*. However, after her time in Germany, Ruth longed to cover more than local news. She wanted to be part of the big events that were shaping the world. So in 1935, she applied for and received a writing fellowship that would pay her to write about anything creative.

She decided to study how women lived under different forms of government. She would go to Germany to observe women in a fascist society and then Russia to study women in a communist society.

When she told her editor at the *Herald Tribune*, he was impressed. He invited Ruth to be the paper's special foreign correspondent while she was in Europe. If she came across important stories, she could send them to the *Herald Tribune*.

Ruth was thrilled. She had a fellowship *and* a journalism assignment. Her dream of being a writer was coming true.

Her parents reacted differently.

"Why do you have to go back to Germany?" her mother wept. "They can kill you."

"I'll be careful," Ruth answered.

Her mother didn't understand why she couldn't just settle down. "It's time you got married already."

"There are things I want to do first, Mama."

Ruth left for Europe with one small suitcase, her portable typewriter, and her camera. What would she find in Germany? Was she really in as much danger as her parents feared? She lifted her chin and straightened her shoulders. She would be professional, get her story, and then go home. That would keep her safe. Wouldn't it?

## Fascism and Communism

A fascist government is ruled by a dictator who has total power. Hitler was Germany's dictator from 1933 to 1945. Under fascism, anyone who opposes or criticizes the leader faces severe punishment.

Communists believe that all property and resources should be shared equally in a society. Russia, which became the Soviet Union in 1922, had a communist government from 1917 to 1991. In practice, the government controlled the country's resources, making top government officials rich while many ordinary people suffered from poverty.

Both communism and fascism contrast with democracy, which focuses on individuals. Citizens of democracies are encouraged to own businesses and property and to make their own decisions. This results in success for some and struggle for others.

\*\*\*

Before heading to Germany's capital, Berlin, Ruth stopped in Cologne to see her friends. First, she went to her friend Miriam's house. In a voice filled with fear, Miriam's mother whispered that Miriam had left, but she didn't know where she'd gone. Ruth hoped she was somewhere safe. The Herzes had moved to the Netherlands earlier that year, to Ruth's relief.

She had asked Johann to meet her at her hotel. Instead of waiting for him there, though, she took a walk to clear her head.

Red flags with black swastikas were draped on buildings and hung from windows. She saw signs on storefronts: NO JEWS ALLOWED.

Ruth entered a bookshop. It was crowded with people browsing and chatting. Suddenly, Hitler's voice came over a loudspeaker. Everyone stood at attention as Hitler ranted about the Jews and about how other European countries had tried to destroy Germany.

Ruth left the shop feeling as if she had been attacked. Outside, she saw officers in black uniforms and shiny black boots—members of the Gestapo, the new German secret police. They herded a group of adults and children down the street, forcing them to walk in the gutter. Some stood tall but others were bent over in exhaustion. A crowd gathered to watch the scene.

Ruth asked someone where these people were being taken. He responded that they were Jews on their way to a work camp.

Ruth wanted to do something, but she knew she couldn't stop the armed Gestapo officers. Instead she headed for her hotel. Her heart was so heavy that she felt it might drop out of her chest.

Back in her room, a knock on the door set her heart trembling. Johann walked in and took her hand.

She snatched it back. She was still angry about what she'd seen.

"Johann, what is happening here is terrible—frightening—a nightmare."

Johann tried to convince her that she was overreacting. He said Hitler had created jobs, especially in the military. He claimed that Hitler's leadership had given Germans hope.

Ruth looked at him suspiciously. "Johann, did you become a Nazi?"

He wouldn't meet her eyes. He admitted he'd joined the Nazi Party. He felt it was the only way he could get a teaching job. "I would have been unemployed. How could I support my mother?"

Ruth had no time for his excuses. "Get out!" she exploded. She never saw him again.

Chapter 6

# A Family Reunion

Ruth left Germany with a sinking heart. Everything she had seen and heard there convinced her that Jews were in terrible danger.

Her next stop was Poland. She had promised her mother that she would try to see her relatives in Beremlya, the shtetl about an hour from Warsaw where her mother had been born.

Her train pulled into Warsaw at midnight. As she got off, a man wearing shabby clothes, a cap pulled low on his head, and torn boots approached her.

"You are Ruth," he said in Yiddish. "I am Yankel, your mother's cousin, Mirel's son. Come quickly." He picked up her suitcase, typewriter, and camera case and led her to a horse and cart. "Jump in. And hide under the hay," he said.

"Can't I sit up front with you?"

"Not safe." He covered her with a coarse blanket.

The blanket smelled like horse manure, and the hay tickled her skin. As the wagon bumped along, Ruth's mind filled with questions. Why was Yankel afraid for her safety? Or was he afraid for himself? Ruth knew that Poland could be a dangerous place

## Pogroms

Pogrom is a Russian word meaning "to destroy violently." Starting in the 1800s, the term was used to describe attacks on Jews by non-Jews in Eastern Europe. Local police officers and government officials often helped organize these attacks. Thousands of Jews were killed in pogroms. Others saw their homes and businesses destroyed. Many Jews immigrated to countries like the United States and Canada hoping to escape this violence.

for Jews to live. Years ago, her grandparents had fled to the United States because of pogroms—attacks on Jews.

It was two o'clock in the morning when Yankel pulled into a small dirt-filled courtyard. "Wake up, everybody," he called. "Gussie's daughter has come."

Ruth got off the cart, brushing bits of hay from her hair and clothes. Suddenly, she was surrounded by aunts, uncles, and cousins she'd never met. Her great-aunt Mirel pulled her into her small cottage, and everyone followed, bombarding Ruth with questions. How were her mother and grandmother? What was Ruth doing in Poland? Why wasn't she married? Weren't there good men in America?

Ruth felt as if she had stepped back in time. The women wore long-sleeved dresses and covered their heads in kerchiefs; the men wore loose pants secured with rope. The barefoot children stared at Ruth as if she were from another planet. Yet even with all their differences, she felt a link in the shape of their faces, the warmth in their eyes.

She turned to a young girl named Hannah. "Do you go to school?"

"I went only enough to read and write."

"What do you want to be?"

Hannah lowered her eyes. "They'll pick somebody for me to marry, and I'll have children."

Ruth suppressed a sigh. If Hannah lived in New York, she would have more options.

"We have to find a dowry for Hannah," Mirel said. "If not for the money your father sends us every month—God should only bless him and keep him alive till a hundred and twenty—we would starve."

So this was where the packages of clothes and the money had gone all these years.

They were interrupted by a pounding on the door. Yankel opened it, and two policemen pushed into the crowded space.

"Who is she?" The taller one pointed at Ruth. "Someone has reported [seeing] a stranger."

"She's my sister's grandchild," Mirel said. "She came from America to see us."

The police officers looked Ruth up and down and then noticed her typewriter and camera. Ruth worried that the equipment made her look suspicious. Perhaps the officers thought she was a spy.

The tall policeman demanded to see her passport. Ruth took it from her bag and handed it to him. Next he emptied her suitcase and examined every piece of clothing.

He eyed her with distrust. "What are you doing here?"

"I am a student and a tourist," Ruth responded, hoping the word *student* would explain her typewriter and camera.

"We want you out of here in one hour," the tall policeman ordered. "If you're not gone by then, we'll come back and arrest you."

When the officers had left, Yankel told Ruth, "You better go immediately."

Ruth looked at the family. It was clear they were all terrified. Ruth's heart was pounding, and she found it hard to breathe.

Hannah grasped her arm. "Don't go yet!"

Ruth embraced her. Her heart ached. *I can go home to America, but she's trapped. They're all trapped.* She walked to the table where the officers had spilled the contents of her suitcase. Rummaging through clothes, she pulled out her favorite dress and two sets of underwear, which she gave to Hannah.

Hannah clutched them to her chest. "For my wedding!"

Ruth stuffed the rest of her things back into the suitcase, kissed Hannah and the others, and followed Yankel to the courtyard. Once again, she hid under the hay while he drove the wagon to the Warsaw train station. Her muscles ached from lying scrunched in the cart.

Once she'd boarded the train to Moscow, she tried to make sense of the darkness she was leaving behind. Her family lived in terror. What would happen to them?

Her next stop was the Soviet Union, a nation cloaked in secrecy. She wondered what she would find there—more terror, or a genuine chance to learn and explore? Either way, she sensed that this trip would change the course of her life.

Chapter 7

# An Amazing Opportunity

Ruth wanted to find out as much as she could about the Soviet Arctic. She knew the Russians were exploring and conducting scientific experiments there. But they'd been extremely secretive about their activities. Ruth was especially curious about the women who worked in the Arctic.

In Moscow, she arranged to meet Professor Otto Schmidt, who was in charge of the Soviet Union's Arctic ventures.

She told him of her plan to document what women were doing in the Arctic. Why did they go there? How did they deal with the dangers and hardships? And were they treated differently from the men?

Professor Schmidt explained that women were going north for the same reasons as men—to build new cities, to explore, and especially to earn more money. He walked to the large Arctic map on the wall. "Here's Igarka." He pointed to a town in Siberia. Five years ago, he said, no one had lived there. Now it was a busy lumber town. "And," he added, "the leader of Igarka is a woman."

Ruth stared at him in amazement. A woman was running a lumber town in the Arctic? That was a story she would love to write.

"You know," said Professor Schmidt, "we've never sent a foreign correspondent to the Arctic. But we can send you." He offered to pay for Ruth's transportation expenses and telegram fees.

Ruth walked out of Professor Schmidt's office in a daze. She felt like jumping up and down but contained herself. She couldn't believe her luck. She was being sent to someplace no foreign reporter—man or woman—had ever gone. She was only twenty-four years old, and she was making history!

Ruth spent the next few days preparing for her trip. The remote Arctic would be a physically challenging environment. Other correspondents gave her warm clothing, fur-lined mittens, and even chocolate. One woman brought her two hot water bottles.

## Russia at a Glance

For hundreds of years, Russia was ruled by a tsar who was the head of state and the head of the church. In 1917, at the end of World War I, a revolution broke out. The tsar was overthrown, and a communist group led by Vladimir Lenin came to power. The Union of Soviet Socialist Republics (USSR), also known as the Soviet Union, was established soon afterward. It included Russia, Belorussia, Ukraine, and the Georgian, Azerbaijan, and Armenian republics. It was the first communist country in the world.

Under communism, the government owns the land, farms, and factories. When Lenin died in 1922, Joseph Stalin took over. Stalin was a brutal dictator who jailed his opponents and killed millions of his own people. He ruled until his death in 1953. In 1991, the Soviet Union broke apart into separate countries again.

## Communication in the Arctic

Long-distance communication in the Siberian Arctic was difficult, expensive, and slow. Mail often took months to arrive at its destination. Storms could knock out telephone wires. The quickest way to send messages—including Ruth's stories—was by radio or telegram. Telegrams were sent as coded electric signals over a wire. They had to be relayed from one telegraph station to the next. When Ruth's editors told her parents they wouldn't hear from her for months, they were telling them not to worry: she was safe, but not always able to communicate with them.

She added notebooks, typing paper, pencils, and film for her camera.

She still planned to write stories for the *Herald Tribune*. Her plan was to transmit her articles from radio stations in the Arctic to the *Herald Tribune*'s correspondent in Moscow, who would forward them to New York and Paris. Meanwhile, the *Herald Tribune* informed her parents that they might not hear from her for months. Ruth pictured her father's face. He'd be tense with worry. And her mother would say that they shouldn't have let her go. Then her father would answer that no one could have stopped her. And he'd be right.

\*\*\*

Early the next morning, Ruth was at the airport carrying her duffel bag and typewriter, her camera slung over her shoulder. She and seven Russian men climbed into a small plane that would take them part of the way to the Arctic.

During the flight, Ruth spread a map on her lap and followed the plane's route. As the plane bounced and swayed, she looked down at mile after mile of earth and trees and wheat fields that stretched to the horizon.

It took two weeks to reach Igarka. Ruth often had to stop in towns and villages along the way to wait for her plane to refuel or to switch to a new plane. On one leg of the journey, she even flew in a mail plane with an open cockpit. The people she met wondered what a young American journalist was doing so far from home. Ruth spoke to them in Russian. She told them she was there to learn about their lives. Every time she entered a new time zone, Ruth set her watch ahead one hour. It made her realize how huge the Soviet Union was.

## *Siberia and the Soviet Arctic*

Siberia is an extensive region that has been part of Russia since the late 1700s. It is located within the Soviet Arctic, an area of about 2,100,000 square miles (5,500,000 square kilometers). The region spans nine of Russia's eleven time zones, from Norway to the Bering Strait. It boasts a wealth of mineral and natural resources. In the 1920s, the Soviet Union began exploring the area and developing its resources.

***

Ruth's first impression of Igarka, a town of 5,000 people, was of wooden houses stained brown by weather and smoke. Logs floated downstream into the harbor, where ships loaded lumber.

Life in the Arctic was brutal. Summer temperatures were often as high as 80 degrees Fahrenheit (26.7 degrees Celsius), and

in winter, they could drop as low as -50 degrees Fahrenheit (-46 degrees Celsius). In summer, the sun shone for almost twenty-four hours, but in winter it was dark most of the day.

There was no hotel in Igarka, so Ruth stayed in a small, simply furnished room in an administrative building. After unpacking and changing into comfortable clothes, Ruth set out to explore the town she had traveled 11,000 miles (17,700 km) to visit. It was late summer and the sky was bright, even though it was 10 p.m. Ruth stumbled along a muddy path, tripping over tree stumps, until she saw lights ahead. She climbed down a hill and emerged from the forest onto a brightly lit wharf. Hundreds of men and women were loading lumber onto ships with English, Norwegian, and Danish names. Ruth heard a dozen languages. This lively scene of people from so many countries fascinated her. And the next morning, she would meet Igarka's mayor. She could hardly wait.

*** 

The mayor was a thin woman in her forties, with closely cropped black hair. She didn't seem interested in talking to Ruth. She gave short, impatient answers to Ruth's questions.

Ruth was disappointed. She hadn't learned anything new. She decided to talk to another woman leader. So she met with Maria Mitrofanovna Khrenikova, who was in charge of raising fresh vegetables and livestock at the Polar State Farm.

Maria, a short, round woman wearing an old sweater and skirt, met Ruth at the door of her home. She had a soft manner, but

when she spoke, it was to demand answers from Ruth. "You are searching. What are you looking for?"

"I want to understand the world, especially this new world in the Arctic." Ruth explained her project and asked Maria about the polar farm she was running.

"Come and see it." Maria led Ruth outdoors and into the greenhouses where she was growing vegetables. Maria explained that she was experimenting to see what would grow in the Arctic. "We try about five hundred experiments a year, and so far about thirty or forty have been successful." The successful crops included turnips, which were loaded with vitamin C. They could prevent scurvy, a disease caused by a lack of vitamins and sunshine.

Ruth was impressed. People needed vegetables to stay healthy, and it was hard to grow anything in the Arctic's frozen soil. This woman was meeting the challenge. Here was something Ruth could write about.

\*\*\*

About half of Igarka's people were settlers. The other half were prisoners. The prisoners lived in their own homes and had jobs but could not leave Igarka until their sentences were up.

One prisoner told Ruth that she and her husband had lost their farm when the government took control of it. "I had a cow there and I milked her every day," she said. "Here I have nothing."

Another woman cut in. "Before the revolution, she and her husband had a farm in Siberia. But she doesn't tell you they were bad to their workers."

Ruth wasn't sure what to believe. Some prisoners had broken the law by stealing or harming other people. But others were political prisoners whose only crime was criticizing the government. Ruth could see that the prisoners hated living in Igarka.

The second woman was a settler who'd chosen to come there. She told Ruth, "Me, I'm young. I love it here. I'm building for the whole world."

Ruth saw that each woman in the Arctic had a unique experience. After only a week, she sent her first story to her newspaper's Moscow bureau, which then forwarded it to New York. But she was only getting started.

Chapter 8

# Yakutsk

When Ruth returned to New York, she wrote four articles for the *Herald Tribune* about what she'd learned on her trip. She also traveled around the United States and Canada giving speeches about the injustices she had witnessed in Hitler's Germany.

In the spring of 1936, Professor Schmidt invited her to come back to Siberia. He suggested that she live in the Russian port town of Yakutsk and find out how the Soviets were treating the region's Indigenous Yakut population. Ruth knew that the Yakuts mostly raised cattle, horses, and reindeer. She jumped at the chance to learn more.

When Ruth told her parents that she had been invited back to the Soviet Arctic, they were resigned. "No use trying to stop you," her father said, while her mother shook her head and sighed.

Ruth traveled to Moscow and then rode the Trans-Siberian Railway across European Russia and Siberia to Irkutsk. From there, she took a seaplane to Yakutsk.

Ruth sat in the plane's cabin, under the wing. It was so dark inside that Ruth felt as if she'd entered the belly of a whale. The plane stopped in several towns along the way before arriving in Yakutsk on the third day.

With a population of 25,000 people, Yakutsk was larger than Igarka. Ruth stayed in a local politician's four-room cottage.

Ruth had heard that political prisoners lived in Yakutsk. But when she asked where to find them, people claimed they didn't know. So she arranged to meet with someone who *had* to know: Andrei Petrovich Carosin, the head of the NKVD—the Soviet secret police. Ruth was excited but also apprehensive as she entered his office. When Carosin greeted her, Ruth didn't waste time.

"Everybody knows you have political prisoners in Yakutsk. I've promised the *Herald Tribune* a story on them."

Carosin smiled. He said she could find political prisoners all over town. "One of them runs the bookshop."

This surprised Ruth. She'd expected a prison.

"We don't have prisons here as they do in capitalist countries," Carosin told her. "We don't have guards or jailers [. . .] Our political exiles are free to live anywhere they choose—in the province to which we send them, of course."

"What happens if they try to escape?"

He laughed. "It's hard to escape from Siberia." The town was surrounded by dense forests. The only way out was by airplane or ship, which the prisoners were not allowed to use. Still, Carosin insisted the prisoners were content.

After Ruth left the NKVD office, she stopped by the bookstore that Carosin had mentioned. It was filled with books, stacked up against the walls, but there were no customers. A tall, stooped man approached her. "I know who you are," he said excitedly in English. "I read about you in the newspaper. It's unbelievable. Almost no one—no foreigners, not even Russians—can get to Yakutsk. And you—a mere woman!"

Ruth ignored that remark.

The man's name was Medved. He was very thin, and his eyes, behind thick glasses, were red-rimmed. His clothes were ragged. Ruth wanted to know about his life as a political prisoner, and Medved was willing to talk to her.

"But not here." He lowered his voice. "Can you come to my apartment this evening? I live right over the store."

Ruth instantly agreed.

"Be very careful," he added. "Make sure no one follows you. It would be very bad for me if the NKVD found out I was talking to you."

\*\*\*

Ruth waited until it was dark and then sneaked back to the bookstore. She left her camera behind but hid a small notebook in her clothes so she could write down what Medved would tell her. Medved was waiting for her at the store. He looked up and down the street to make sure no one had followed her. Then he led her up a flight of rickety stairs to a dimly lit loft.

The only light was a candle in a green bottle on a bare table in a corner of the room. There was a cot in the center of the

room, its four legs stuck in tin cans of water. Ruth remembered stories her father had told of Russians using the water to trap bedbugs.

Medved led Ruth to the table. "Now I will show you how a prisoner of Stalin lives in Yakutsk."

Ruth took out her notebook. When she took notes, she wrote them in tiny squiggly script so that if they were discovered, no one else could read her writing.

Medved's only crime had been criticizing Joseph Stalin, the Soviet Union's leader. The authorities had arrested him and tortured him.

Ruth said, "I was told that political prisoners are not put into prisons."

Medved snorted. "I was in prison for eight years. Then I was exiled to Yakutsk for four years." He told her that there were tens of thousands of prisoners all over Siberia, many of them in prison camps called gulags.

Ruth asked about conditions in Yakutsk. "Is it true that you're free to do whatever work you're suited for?"

Medved shook his head. "They pick the work. They gave me the job in the bookstore because I speak seven languages. [. . .] If

# The Gulag

The Soviet gulag was a system of forced labor camps for criminals and political prisoners. Under Joseph Stalin's dictatorship, people who disagreed with the government were sent to the camps. Conditions were brutal, and many prisoners died from starvation and disease. After Stalin's death in 1953, millions of prisoners were released and the true horror of the camps was revealed.

they let me do my own work, I'd be in the library doing research."
He also said that 80 percent of the people in Yakutsk were sick due
to lack of food and medicine.

By the time Ruth left the apartment, her heart was heavy for
Medved and all the people trapped in this heartless system. She
knew she couldn't change what had happened to him. All she
could do was to tell his story.

## Chapter 9

# A Conversation and a Gift

The days were getting short. Winter was coming. Ruth had interviewed workers, prisoners, and government officials. She had visited Yakut people living in reindeer-skin tents and yurts made of wood and dung. It was time to go home, but first there was one more woman she wanted to interview: a 104-year-old Yakut woman named Marfa who lived on a collective farm. Ruth traveled to the farm with a Yakut politician who would translate the Yakut language into Russian for her.

Marfa lived in a yellow two-room house. Her bronzed face was seamed with wrinkles. She wore dangling gold earrings, a

## *Russia's Many Peoples*

Russia is home to more than 100 ethnic groups. Only about forty very small groups are officially recognized by the Russian government as Indigenous peoples. The Yakut people, who call themselves the Sakha, are one of the larger groups. They live mainly in northeastern Russia.

cotton dress, a scarf tied around her head, and boots made of reindeer hide.

"I am the mother of twenty children," Marfa told her.

Ruth gasped. "Twenty children!"

Marfa leaned forward. "We gave birth like cattle, right on the mud floor [. . .] Nobody knows how many women died at childbirth; nobody knows how many of our babies died."

Marfa had had a difficult life. "I was an orphan. [. . .] My uncle took me to his house. I worked for him without pay, though he was a rich man, and he married me off very young [. . .] You have children?" Marfa asked Ruth.

Ruth replied that she didn't.

"You sick?" Marfa asked.

Ruth looked around the little house. They were sitting on straight-backed chairs around a table with a white cloth. Suddenly she felt as if she were back at the kitchen table in her parents' apartment in Brooklyn, and her mother was questioning her about settling down and having a family. She marveled how the lives of these two women, worlds and cultures apart, revolved around the same thing—being mothers.

"If I had children," Ruth said, "I would be home nursing them, bathing them. I wouldn't be in your house today."

"Don't have twenty children," Marfa chuckled. "But don't wait too long."

Ruth asked about Marfa's children.

Tears rolled down the woman's wrinkled cheeks. "All of them are dead. Only their children are alive."

Ruth took her hand, reflecting on Marfa's long life. "She had lived through a hundred years of Russian history," Ruth wrote later, "[. . .] bearing twenty children, raising them, feeding them, healing them when they were sick, then burying them all."

Marfa went into the second room. She came back with an object that Ruth thought looked like a small Viking boat. She realized it was a cradle was made of birch bark and carved to fit a baby's body. It had thin leather straps to tie it to a reindeer's antlers when the family was traveling, plus reindeer-bone bars the mother would hold to rock the baby. Ruth discovered a wooden pan under a hole, with a drain leading to a birch bark potty. Yakut babies would never have to wear diapers.

"You like it?" Marfa asked.

"It's a wonderful piece of engineering," Ruth marveled.

Marfa handed it to her. "It is for you."

Ruth was taken aback. "Oh no, no. I really can't accept it."

The translator told her, "You would humiliate her if you don't take it."

Ruth grasped Marfa's hand. "I will treasure this cradle all my life, and if I ever have children . . ."

Marfa smiled.

\*\*\*

Ruth packed her notebooks with the interviews she'd conducted and the film with all the pictures she had taken. And she took the cradle that Marfa had given her back to the United States.

Traveling in the Arctic had been a great adventure. Ruth wanted to keep traveling and exploring. Most of all, she wanted to use words and images to capture events in the chaotic world that she feared was on the verge of war.

When Ruth returned to the United States, she wrote a book about her experiences. Her book *I Went to the Soviet Arctic* was published on September 1, 1939. That same day, German troops invaded Poland. World War II had begun.

## Chapter 10

# Alaska

R uth was now a well-established writer and speaker. In the spring of 1941, her editor at the *Herald Tribune* suggested that Ruth go to Alaska. "We'd like you to do a series of articles on how we're preparing for war up there. Alaska's going to become very important."

So far, the United States had stayed out of the war. But its European allies—Great Britain and France—wanted the US military's help fighting Germany, which was taking over more and more European countries. Tension was also high between the United States and Japan, one of Germany's allies. And Alaska, on the coast of the Pacific Ocean, was very close to Japan. If conflict broke out, Alaska could be a target.

Ruth's editor suggested that Ruth go to Washington to meet with Harold Ickes, the secretary of the interior. Since Alaska was a territory, not a state, Secretary Ickes's department was in charge of it.

Secretary Ickes was a kindly looking man who immediately put Ruth at ease.

"Don't go to Alaska for the *Herald Tribune*," he said. "Go for me. I read your book on the Soviet Arctic. I want you to do

# *Alaska*

The United States government bought Alaska from Russia in 1867 for $7 million. In 1898, gold was discovered there, bringing thousands of miners and settlers to the area. In 1912, Alaska became a US territory, and on January 3, 1959, it became the forty-ninth state.

something similar [. . .] Stay about a year. Take a couple of cameras and even a movie camera."

Surprised but intrigued, Ruth agreed. She had come for an interview and left with a full-time job.

\*\*\*

In 1941, Alaska was a vast expanse of land with very few inhabitants. There were thirty thousand native people and thirty thousand settlers. The land was wild, rough, and largely empty— just the kind of challenge Ruth loved.

Ruth traveled all over Alaska. She took hundreds of pictures to document the lives of the people she met and the landscapes she saw. She explored the territory's vast forests, majestic mountain ranges, roaring rivers, and rugged coastlines.

Ruth was especially interested in Alaska's Indigenous peoples. She admired how they adapted to the harsh climate, using natural materials to survive. They turned the bones, fur, skins, and meat of animals into clothing, housing, and food.

Ruth sent regular reports to Secretary Ickes. She knew that if war with Japan broke out, Japan could easily attack the Aleutian Islands off the coast of Alaska. The islands were home to the Aleuts, a seal-hunting people. She wrote to Secretary Ickes that the Aleuts were in harm's way. Secretary Ickes sent the Coast Guard to evacuate them. Ruth met the Aleuts and helped them resettle near the city of Juneau, where they would be safer.

She visited towns and villages all over the territory, including Indigenous communities where she made many friends. As she had in Siberia, she experienced the summer's endless sunlight and the

## Peoples of Alaska

Dozens of Indigenous peoples live in Alaska. They include the Inuit, the Yupik, and the Aleut, who all speak related languages. Ruth called the people she met "Eskimos," which was the term most Americans used at the time to refer to the Inuit and the Yupik. (This term is no longer used.) Many Inuit and Yupik people have carried on traditions such as walrus hunting into the twenty-first century.

winter's freezing temperatures and darkness. She flew with bush pilots in small planes that bounced like corks through stormy air.

Before coming to Alaska, Ruth had always been in a hurry to move from one task or adventure to the next. In Alaska, she learned to have patience. Trains were often late because the tracks were blocked by snow or ice. Flights were canceled because of storms. Ruth often heard the term "weapers," meaning "weather permitting," as she waited days and even weeks for a flight. She used the extra time to write her reports, read, and spend time with her Indigenous friends. She took pictures of hunters and of mothers with their children.

One day a group invited her to join a walrus hunt. Ruth knew this was a great honor. She was excited but nervous. The thought of killing an animal sickened her, yet she understood that the hunters depended on the animals. People used their meat for food, their oil for fuel, and their hides for clothing and tents.

The group set out in a small boat, steering around ice floes. As they neared the hunting area, the men put on white parkas to

blend in with the ice. Eventually they spotted a walrus stretched
out on a floe.

Ruth admired the walrus's long tusks, resting on the ice like
curved ivory swords. Its thick skin rippled in deep folds around its
shoulders, and a band of stiff, quill-like whiskers gave it a comic
appearance that made her smile. She had brought her movie
camera with her. She lifted it and began filming.

A hunter flung his harpoon into the walrus's body. Then, using a rope, he pulled the animal alongside the boat and towed it to a large ice floe.

As the hunters celebrated, Ruth reminded herself that they had killed this magnificent creature not for sport or profit but for survival. She continued filming as one of the men cut through the animal's skin with a sharp knife. He removed the blubber and handed pieces to everyone, including Ruth. She knew it would be rude to refuse to eat it. Taking a deep breath, she bit into the fatty substance, chewed, and managed to swallow.

\*\*\*

Ruth stayed in Alaska for eighteen months. She filled dozens of notebooks with her impressions. And she took as many pictures as she could. She felt that photographs reveal the soul. While she didn't want to romanticize Alaska, she did want to show the lives of the people who called it home—especially those who were working to preserve its resources and beauty.

Chapter 11

# A Dangerous Mission

**R**uth returned to Washington in the fall of 1943. She was ready to head to New York, get her own apartment, and continue working as a journalist. But Secretary Ickes asked her to remain in Washington and work for him.

The United States had entered World War II in December 1941, after Japanese planes bombed the naval base at Pearl Harbor in Hawaii. The US government had declared war on Japan, and then Japan's ally, Germany, declared war on the United States. Ruth was following the war news closely. She read about Germany's persecution of Jews and worried about her relatives in Poland. Her father's attempts to contact them failed. There had been no word from them in over two years.

## *Lost Relatives*

After the war, Ruth learned that all her relatives in Poland had died in the Holocaust. The only surviving member of that side of the family was Ruth's cousin Dvora, who had moved to Palestine in the 1930s.

Ruth was frustrated and angry. She knew many Americans were against bringing more immigrants—especially Jewish immigrants—into the country. And without pressure from the public, politicians didn't feel compelled to take action. But Ruth felt the US government should be

doing much more to help Jews escape the Nazis.

Finally, in 1944, President Franklin D. Roosevelt decided to bring one thousand refugees, most of them Jewish, from Italy to the United States. And when she heard that the president asked Secretary Ickes to take charge of the project, Ruth saw her chance to get involved.

At her next meeting with Secretary Ickes, she said, "Mr. Secretary, these refugees are going to be terrified, traumatized. Somebody has to hold their hands."

Secretary Ickes was sitting at his desk, looking tired and worried. But when Ruth spoke, his expression brightened. "Of course. I'm going to send you. You're a young woman. You're Jewish. There will be a lot of women and children." He told her she would be going as the president's representative. "It's top secret. We'll have to make you a general."

Ruth stared at him in amazement. "Me? A general?"

"You'll be flying in a military plane. If you're shot down and the Nazis capture you, as a civilian, they can kill you as a spy. But as a general, according to the Geneva Convention, you must be given shelter and food, and kept alive."

Ruth gulped. Until now, she hadn't thought about the danger of this mission. Yet she lifted her chin. "Thank you, Mr. Secretary. This will be the most important assignment of my life."

Chapter 12

# Onboard the *Henry Gibbons*

When Ruth reached Naples, Italy, she was horrified by what she saw. Naples had been liberated by American troops, but it had been heavily bombed by the Germans. Half-destroyed buildings stood like skeletons. Ragged children played on piles of rubble in the streets.

An army driver took Ruth to the dock where she would meet the refugees going to the United States. Ruth saw soldiers marching off troop ships, carrying guns and combat gear, and then boarding trucks that would take them to the battlefronts in northern Italy and other parts of Europe.

A young navy lieutenant helped her get into a small boat that took her to the larger ship the refugees had boarded. "There she is." He pointed to huge vessel with a black smokestack and elevated guns to shoot down enemy planes. "It's an Army troop transport, the *Henry Gibbons*." The ship held not only the refugees but about a thousand wounded soldiers on their way to US hospitals. The *Henry Gibbons* would travel with a convoy of other US warships.

The lieutenant signaled to a crew member on the ship, who

# The Convoy

The *Henry Gibbons* was a US Army transport ship carrying soldiers, refugees, and German prisoners of war being sent to the United States. It was part of a large convoy of troop ships, destroyers, cruisers, and cargo ships. Additional vessels joined the convoy when it entered the Mediterranean Sea, where German submarines and bombers patrolled. President Roosevelt ordered that if the convoy was attacked, protection of the *Henry Gibbons* was the warships' first priority.

dropped a rope ladder down the side. Then he looked at Ruth and frowned.

He doubted she could climb the rope ladder her white suit, white gloves, and wide red straw hat. He had a soldier loan her a pair of pants.

Ruth pulled the pants over her skirt. Then she began climbing the rope ladder. She fought to keep her balance as the ladder swung and pitched against the hull of the ship. She clutched the ropes so tightly that they dug into her hands. The water below looked dark and angry. Ruth swallowed her queasiness and concentrated on climbing. When she reached the top, a sailor hauled her onto the ship's deck.

As Ruth struggled to catch her breath, she heard a man shout, "It's Eleanor Roosevelt!"

Ruth laughed as refugees crowded around her. Then she sobered. She was surrounded by men in ragged shorts, women in threadbare skirts and blouses. Some people had cloth or newspaper tied around their feet. Children, mostly barefoot and in rags, looked up at her with haunted eyes.

Ruth headed to the bridge to meet the captain. He explained that this was the first time the ship had carried refugees. He made it clear that the refugees shouldn't have any contact with the sailors. Socializing with civilians could be too distracting for the crew. The refugees were supposed to stay in the forward holds—near the front of the ship—while the soldiers stuck to the holds in the stern, or the back. Ruth could go anywhere on the ship, though.

There were 982 refugees aboard the *Henry Gibbons*. They came from eighteen different countries and spoke eighteen different languages. While 874 were Jewish, seventy-three were Catholic, twenty-eight were Greek Orthodox, and seven were Protestant. President Roosevelt had wanted to include people from several different religions so that the project wouldn't seem like a strictly Jewish-focused mission. The oldest refugee was an eighty-year-old man, and the youngest was an infant.

## *Many Backgrounds*

Nazi Germany was responsible for the murder of at least six million Jews. The Nazis also killed about five million non-Jews as part of their program to "purify" Europe. These other victims included disabled people, gay people, and members of various racial, ethnic, and religious minorities. For instance, many Polish Catholics were targeted for violence after Germany invaded Poland. And anyone from any background who spoke out against the Nazis risked death.

These were the people Ruth was here to help in any way she could. That would mean more than simply easing their fears while they traveled. It would mean listening to their stories and then sharing those stories with an American audience. This was the first group of survivors coming to the United States. Perhaps when Americans could put names and faces to the atrocities they had been reading about, they'd be more willing to support refugees.

After she'd gotten settled in her cabin and changed into a skirt, Ruth went up on deck. There, she joined a group sitting on the ledge of a covered metal hatch. She introduced herself and explained that she worked for the US government. She spoke in German and Yiddish, languages that most of the refugees understood.

"Are you FBI?" said a man.

"Me? FBI? Good heavens, no."

"So what *are* you doing on this ship?" asked someone else.

Ruth looked up at them, making eye contact with as many people as possible. "When we get to America," Ruth explained, "I will report to my boss [. . .] and he will report to the president, the cabinet, and Congress. I would like them to know who you are, what kind of people you are. What you've gone through to survive."

"We're all kinds of people," said a small man named Otto Presser. He spoke with broad, theatrical gestures. "Big and little, some once rich, some not so rich, and now all the same—poor."

Ruth smiled. The man was charming and seemed to be well liked by the others. She later learned that he had been a song and dance entertainer in Vienna.

Leo Mirkovic, a skeletal man in silk pajamas that had once been white but were gray with wear, told her that before the war he had been an opera singer. She learned that others were professional musicians and singers.

"People in America are just beginning to learn of the atrocities that Hitler and his people have committed," she told them. "You will be the first group of refugees the people of the United States will see. You are the living witnesses."

The crowd was silent. Then a tall, thin man with sad eyes spoke up. "You're a woman. How can I tell you the things they did to me—the dirty, filthy, obscene things?"

"It's your story, it's your experiences that are important—not how they affect me," Ruth told him. "Maybe if the world knows what you suffered, maybe we'll be able to rescue more people."

The clang of metal made them turn as the ship's huge steel anchor was lifted.

"We're sailing!" a few refugees called.

Everyone rushed to the rail. Some waved farewell to Europe. Others wept. Warships maneuvered into formation around the *Henry Gibbons* as the convoy headed into the blue waters of the Mediterranean Sea.

\*\*\*

Dinner was served in the ship's galley. Ruth watched as the refugees gazed in awe at the tables loaded with mounds of boiled potatoes, salmon salad, frankfurters and goulash, loaves of sliced bread, and platters of cookies. Ruth saw some of the children hide frankfurters in their shirts and then rush out of the galley. Ruth realized they were saving food in case they didn't get another meal for a long time.

A man turned to Ruth. "So much food! In the camp, all they gave us was dirty hot water."

Later, Ruth went back up on deck. The sun was low in the sky, painting the water surface a molten gold. She closed her eyes and breathed in salty spray. Ruth remained at the rail until the sun sank below the horizon. Then she returned to her cabin, exhausted and excited, wondering what the next few days would bring.

Chapter 13

# At Sea

As the *Henry Gibbons* sailed into the Mediterranean Sea, the mood on board became tense. This was the most dangerous part of the trip. German submarines (U-boats) and war planes patrolled these waters looking for Allied ships to sink. Every morning, alarm bells rang for an air-raid drill. Everyone put on life jackets, and the crewmen hurried to their battle stations. At night, there were no lights, and no one went on deck.

On the third night after leaving Naples, Ruth woke up with a start. Bells were ringing, and she heard footsteps pounding outside her cabin. The loudspeaker crackled to life. "Enemy planes overhead," a voice said in German and English. "Crew and gunners to battle stations. Civilian personnel and wounded soldiers, don life jackets but do not move. Remain in your bunks."

Ruth jumped out of bed. She pulled on a sweater, slacks, shoes, and her life jacket and ran to be with the refugees. She hurried through the causeway, holding on to the wall to keep from falling as the ship rocked from side to side. Then she climbed down the steep ladder into the hold. She knew the rest of the convoy would try to protect the *Henry Gibbons*. Still, could the ship withstand an attack?

She fought back a wave of fear, forcing herself to focus on the refugees. As she entered the hold, she was struck by an eerie silence. She looked at the tiers of bunks lining the cabin. Everyone had on their life jackets and lay absolutely still. Even the babies were quiet. She walked down the aisle talking softly to people, patting some on the arm, taking the hands of others. Suddenly, the silence was broken by the *rat-a-tat-tat* of the ship's antiaircraft and

machine guns shooting at the German planes. Applause rippled through the cabin.

The ship's alarm sounded the all clear. Ruth sighed with relief. The danger was over, at least for now.

Ruth left the refugees' cabin and went to the soldiers' holds.

Men were shouting in fear and anger. "It's because of those lousy Jews!" one soldier screamed. "That's why they're attacking us." Others echoed him.

Ruth shot back that, first of all, the refugees weren't all Jews. "A refugee can be anyone who's homeless, anyone who's displaced." She told the soldiers about what these people had been through. The soldiers listened in silence. She could tell that she hadn't changed their minds. This troubled her almost as much as the German planes that had just passed overhead.

•🌿•

Chapter 14

# Story and Song

**R**uth was in the ship's sick bay chatting with passengers. "Did you give birth on the ship?" she asked a woman named Olga who was nursing her baby.

Olga laughed. "No, he was born in an American jeep." She explained that she and her family had been part of the convoy of vehicles taking refugees to the ship. The soldiers made a bed for her in the back of the Jeep using mattresses and an army cot. When Olga's labor pains began, the driver pulled over to the side of the road, and Olga delivered a healthy baby boy.

The refugees in the other vehicles had hugged each other and cried, "It's an omen. It's a good omen. It's a new life on the road to the Promised Land."

Olga stroked her baby's dark hair. She told Ruth that the soldiers had named him "International Harry."

Ruth kissed "International Harry" and went to write up Olga's story.

\*\*\*

Ruth spoke to the refugees in German and Yiddish. But some spoke neither language. She asked the captain for permission to conduct an English class on the deck. He arranged to have a blackboard set up, and Ruth started teaching.

The Mediterranean sun bathed the deck in gold. People sat on the metal floor, enjoying the warmth and the fresh sea air as they listened eagerly to the American woman's lessons. Slowly, word by word, they began to communicate in English.

When they weren't in class, Ruth listened to the refugees' stories. She heard tales of unbearable suffering in prisons and concentration camps. People told her about losing their families: parents, siblings, and children. Others related feats of unbelievable courage: carrying their children over steep mountains to reach safety, hiding in the forests or in brave people's homes or barns. Ruth wrote page after page of notes and took hundreds of pictures.

"For me, the invitation from President Roosevelt came almost

too late," said Manya Hartmayer, a tall, thin young woman with green eyes in a delicate face. "I was in five concentration camps."

"How old are you, Manya?" Ruth asked.

"I am young, but my heart is two hundred years old. I don't know where my family is [. . .] See this shirt?" She pointed to the man's dark cotton shirt she wore. "It was Papa's. He gave it to me when we were still together in the concentration camp in France." She'd eventually been separated from her father and brothers, ending up in another camp. To cheer herself and other prisoners, Manya sang. Ruth would later remember Manya's talent and its ability to bring people together.

*** 

Ruth sat up in bed. The ship's engines had stopped. Something was wrong, but this time there were no bells or alarms—only an eerie silence.

Ruth threw on a robe and went to the cabin door. A military police officer stood outside. "It's a submarine attack," he said. "You must go below and tell the refugees to be absolutely still."

Ruth quickly got dressed and went down into the refugee hold. Her heart was pounding as she pictured torpedoes hurtling through the water, their deadly noses pointed at the ship. She pictured bursts of fire consuming the corridors and water flooding the hold. She shook her head to clear the images.

In the hold, people were lying in their bunks, motionless. Ruth put her finger to her lips to remind them to keep silent. As she had during the air raid scare, she walked between the rows of bunks, touching hands, masking her own fear to comfort others.

When the all-clear sounded, Ruth went back on deck. The ship was still blacked out, but it was moving. Ruth learned that a U-boat had been tailing the convoy but had lost track of them when the ships turned off their engines: another close call. Ruth was relieved, but she was still troubled. She couldn't stop thinking about how many soldiers aboard the *Henry Gibbons* resented and distrusted the refugees. She wished there was something she could do to change this.

The sound of singing floated toward her. Leo Mirkovic was in a circle of men and women sitting on the deck. Ruth walked over to them. As their voices enveloped her, she had an idea. What if a group of refugees put on a performance for the soldiers? It would be a good excuse for the soldiers to meet the refugees and get to know them as real people.

The refugees loved the suggestion. So Ruth jumped to her feet and went up to the bridge. She asked the captain to loosen the rules against soldiers and refugees mingling.

"We've got some wonderful singers. Professionals. I'd like to see the rules relaxed so the refugees can go to the soldiers' deck and put on a show."

The captain thought for a minute, then agreed.

Ruth immediately got to work organizing the show. People volunteered to sing, dance, and play musical instruments.

Ruth wasn't sure how the soldiers would react to her plan. Maybe they would resent her for trying to get them to bond with the refugees. This effort could be a disaster. But she felt she had to try. She couldn't think of any better way to help the sailors see the refugees as real people.

The next day was warm and sunny with a calm sea. The cast rehearsed in the morning, and that afternoon the soldiers came up from the hold. Ruth watched as the deck filled with men in wheelchairs, with heavy casts on their arms or legs. Some leaned on crutches. Behind them came doctors and nurses. They were

joined by pilots who had finished their missions and were on their way home.

The show began. Edith Semjen, a young woman from Yugoslavia, sang "You Are My Sunshine." The soldiers cheered and shouted for more.

Otto Presser sang and danced. Manya sang a Yiddish song with a catch in her voice that brought tears to Ruth's eyes. Next was Eva Bass, who had been a nightclub singer in Paris. She had escaped from a Gestapo prison. Then, with her twelve-year-old son and her baby daughter, she had walked thirty-eight miles (sixty kilometers) through the fighting lines to reach the Allies.

The program finished with Leo Mirkovic singing an aria.

The soldiers stomped and clapped and pleaded for an encore.

The air had turned cool and the water choppy. But no one wanted to leave the deck until, as the sun set, the performers took a final bow.

***

After the show, the atmosphere eased. Ruth watched with delight as soldiers came on deck to talk with the refugees. Some flirted with girls. Others brought chocolate and cookies for the children.

The convoy moved slowly across the Atlantic Ocean, always on the alert for enemy planes and submarines. Although thirty German planes flew over them during the crossing, they were never attacked.

On August 3, 1944, everyone crammed on deck as the *Henry Gibbons* steamed into New York Harbor. People leaned over the rail waving and pointing at the huge statue of a woman holding a torch.

"The greatest day of my life," an old man wept.

Ruth felt like weeping with him. "Mine too."

The rabbi aboard the ship led the Jewish refugees in the Shehecheyanu, the Hebrew prayer of thanks. "As we enter America, remember, we are one people," he said. "We must speak with one voice, with one heart. We must not live with hatred. We must live with love."

Ruth's eyes filled with tears, and her heart swelled with pride. She moved forward and faced the group. "Do you know what it says on the base of the statue? It's a poem by Emma Lazarus, an American Jewish woman."
She recited the lines.

For a moment there was silence. Then a sound like a collective sob moved through the crowd.

\*\*\*

After the ship docked at the pier, Ruth took a taxi home to see her parents. Her mother and father hugged her, kissed her, and cried. Then the three of them sat around the kitchen table. At last Ruth could tell them about her mission. Her parents listened as she spoke of the refugees. Her father looked stricken, his face shadowed with grief.

Ruth didn't blame him. The stories had torn her apart. But her job wasn't done yet. She needed to tell her fellow Americans about the refugees—to make them understand what these people had been through and what kinds of support they needed now.

"Give me your tired, your poor,
Your huddled masses yearning to breathe free,
The wretched refuse of your teeming shore.
Send these, the homeless, tempest-tossed to me,
I lift my lamp beside the golden door!"
—from "The New Colossus" by Emma Lazarus

## Chapter 15

# A Safe Haven

**A** throng of reporters crowded around Ruth. It reminded her of when she'd come home from Germany with her PhD. Only these reporters didn't want to interview her.

They were at the railroad station in Hoboken, New Jersey, waiting for the train that would take them to the refugee camp in Oswego, New York. The refugees were clustered behind Ruth, still in the ragged clothes they had worn on the ship. Around their necks hung cardboard tags that read US ARMY CASUAL BAGGAGE and had identification numbers.

Ruth had chosen ten refugees to meet with the press. She introduced them one by one, who each gave a brief description of their experiences. The tenth was a thin woman from Yugoslavia named Serafina, clutching a nine-year-old son, Milan. Ruth translated as Serafina told how partisans, people fighting the Nazis, had killed her husband because they thought he was a Nazi. The partisans were sorry and took Serafina and her son to the mountains, where they hid from the Germans.

Ruth bent down to the boy. "Milan, what was it like when you were hiding with the Nazis around you?"

"You always had to speak low," Milan whispered. "They were always telling us, 'Shh shh. The Germans will hear you.'"

The train whistle blew. Ruth made sure all the refugees got aboard the train with her before it chugged out of the station. She looked out the window at the reporters, who were still scribbling notes. She hoped they would spread the word about how much the refugees had suffered. She hoped people reading the stories would understand that the refugees only wanted safety and freedom.

The train arrived in Oswego the next morning. People stared out the windows to get a glimpse of their new home.

"A fence! Another fence!" a man gasped.

"It's another concentration camp," said someone else.

"It's an old army post," Ruth said, trying to reassure them. "All army camps in America have fences."

Ruth led the group off the train and onto the camp grounds. The camp stretched from the edge of the town of Oswego down to the shores of Lake Ontario. On one side of a grassy oval parade ground were the white wooden barracks where the refugees would live. On the opposite side were the fancier brick houses where officers had lived and now Ruth and other workers would be housed. The barracks had been turned into small apartments for families and dormitories for the single adults. In the mess hall, long tables were stacked with pitchers of ice-cold milk and coffee, boxes of cereal, loaves of bread, and jars of peanut butter. After breakfast, Ruth accompanied some of the people to their new homes in the barracks. By midmorning, the refugees had relaxed. Children were playing on the grass while their parents strolled around like tourists.

"Come inside," Kitty Kaufman, a young Austrian, called to Ruth from a window. Ruth entered the small apartment and found Kitty holding two cotton bed sheets.

"In the caves of Italy, I used to dream about bed sheets," Kitty said lovingly.

"And I used to dream about a mattress," her husband, Branko, said. "How many years since we've seen a mattress?"

Ruth looked around the small, plain apartment. It was furnished with two metal cots, a small table, two chairs, and a metal locker. But to these people, who'd gone so long without basic human necessities, it was a palace.

***

Oswego was a town of twenty-two thousand people in central New York State, on the banks of Lake Ontario. The residents were descendants of immigrants who had come to America in the late nineteenth and early twentieth centuries from Germany, Ireland, Canada, Poland, and Italy. Most were Roman Catholic, and there was a small Jewish population.

The refugees had to quarantine for a month—staying isolated in case any of them were sick. However, that didn't stop the

## *A Camp Friendship*

"Beecycla. Beecycla."

Geraldine Desens, a tall, brown-haired young woman, braked and looked through the fence at the children pointing to her bicycle. Geri had never seen a refugee before, but she recognized young people who wanted to ride a bike. So she turned to three men standing near her and motioned for them to throw the bike over the fence. Then she ran home and changed into old clothes, hurried back to the camp, and wiggled through a hole under the fence. While the children took turns riding the bike around the parade ground, Geri struck up a conversation with a young woman named Edith Semjen.

"How did you get in?" Edith asked Geri in amazement.

Geri pointed to the hole. "We always got in this way. It's right opposite Big Rock, our swimming area. It's a shortcut for us."

townspeople from reaching out. Ruth received calls every day from locals who wanted to help. They donated clothes and household goods. And young people from town made friends with the kids their age by talking through the fence.

The next day, Ruth called Secretary Ickes and told him how well the refugees were adjusting to their new home. He asked her to remain in the camp until they were settled, and she agreed.

\*\*\*

As the young women walked around the parade ground, Geri asked Edith about her experiences, emphasizing that Edith didn't have to talk about anything that made her uncomfortable.

"I'll talk," Edith said. She told Geri that she was from Yugoslavia. Her brother and her father had been shot by the Germans. Her mother was sent to Italy, where she ended up in a concentration camp. She escaped, was reunited with Edith, and worked with the partisans. Eventually, Edith and her mother had come to America. "And the first day I meet you [. . .] another rebel like me."

Soon Geri had to leave and get to her job as a waitress. She promised to come back—and bring Edith the biggest steak she had ever seen.

Over the next few weeks, the hole that Geri had used to enter the camp got bigger, and more young people from Oswego became friends with the refugees.

Ruth kept busy trying to meet everyone's needs. She had teachers come to the camp to tutor the children. When the thirty-day quarantine period was up, she arranged day passes so the refugees could go into town for six hours at a time, meaning the children could attend schools in town. She had two buildings on the grounds turned into synagogues—one for Orthodox Jews and another for Conservative Jews. She even organized a wedding.

### Chapter 16

# New Beginnings

Strips of sunlight leaked through the bars on the window of the converted army jail that was Ruth's office.

"Ernst and I want to get married," Manya said. She was still wearing her father's old shirt in memory of him.

Ernst put his arm around Manya's shoulder. His long, thin face and haunted eyes made him look older than his twenty-six years. He explained that he and Manya had both lost their families in the war. They wanted to be married as soon as possible.

Ruth wanted to help them, but it would be difficult because they didn't have legal status in the United States.

Ruth promised she would sort it out but asked them to please be patient.

It took a few weeks to get the legal details worked out, but finally Ruth was able to give the couple good news. They could get married after they had blood tests and filled out some papers.

"Can we get married tomorrow?" Manya asked.

Ruth smiled. "I don't see why not."

Manya beamed, but then her smile faded. She gestured at her father's shirt. "But, Ruthie, I have no dress!"

Ruth thought for a minute. Then she picked up the phone. "We're having a wedding tomorrow, Mom. Can you come up and bring the cocktail dress I left in your house? And a veil for the bride?"

\*\*\*

The next day—August 17—was warm, with a gentle breeze blowing off Lake Ontario. Ruth and a few other women picked wildflowers for Manya's bouquet. Then she went to the barracks where her mother was helping Manya get into her dress.

Gussie had crocheted a silk shawl to serve as a veil. She draped the shawl over Manya's hair. Then she fastened a string of pearls around Manya's neck.

The entire camp came to the wedding on the parade ground. The couple stood under a chuppah, a bridal canopy, as the local rabbi conducted the ceremony. As he pronounced Manya and Ernst husband and wife, cries of "Mazel tov!" filled the air.

\*\*\*

The joy of the wedding lifted everyone's spirits. But the war news once again cast its ugly shadow. In March 1944, Germany had invaded Hungary and immediately started deporting Hungarian Jews to concentration camps. People were terrified for their relatives in that country and throughout Europe. And it still wasn't clear what would happen to the refugees when the war was over.

Then in October, two days after Yom Kippur, an important visitor came to the camp.

Eleanor Roosevelt, the president's wife, wanted to meet the refugees.

Ruth knew that Mrs. Roosevelt wrote a newspaper column that ran in papers all over the country. If the president's wife wrote about the refugees, many Americans would pay attention. Some might even begin to see the refugees in a new light.

Mrs. Roosevelt went into every barrack and listened to people tell their stories. Ruth translated for her as the refugees spoke about the horrors they'd lived through and their dreams of making new lives in America.

Next, everyone gathered in the camp auditorium. Mrs. Roosevelt sat beside Ruth as the group's talented singers and performers entertained them. Afterward, Mrs. Roosevelt got up to speak. Although most of the listeners didn't understand English, they responded to her warmth and compassion. She was the president's wife. Maybe she could convince her husband to let them stay in America.

Mrs. Roosevelt wrote her next column about the people at the Oswego camp. "Somehow you feel that if there is any compensation for suffering, it must someday bring them something beautiful in return for all the horrors they have lived through."

Chapter 17

# The Fight to Remain

On April 12, 1945, President Roosevelt died suddenly. When the news broke, the entire camp gathered in the synagogue to recite the Kaddish, the prayer for the dead. Then, led by the rabbi, they walked across the camp to the flagpole, where they raised the American flag and sang "The Star-Spangled Banner."

The refugees were devastated. President Roosevelt had brought them to America. Who would help them now?

\*\*\*

On May 8, 1945, Germany surrendered to the Allies. The war in Europe was finally over. Four months later, on September 9, the war with Japan ended after the United States dropped devastating atomic bombs on the Japanese cities of Hiroshima and Nagasaki.

While people all over the United States rejoiced, the refugees became increasingly fearful. They were still confined to the camp, with uncertain futures. Would they be allowed to remain in the United States or forced to return to Europe? Their families and homes were gone. The places they'd left would no longer feel like home.

Ruth had been working with Eleanor Roosevelt and Secretary Ickes to fight the government agencies that wanted to send the refugees back to Europe. She traveled to New York to talk to her journalist friends at the *Herald Tribune* and the *New York Times*, asking them to write articles about the refugees and what they had been through.

Her colleagues did as she asked, but their articles didn't change many minds. Popular opinion was still against accepting Jewish refugees.

Ruth returned to the camp and assembled everyone in the auditorium. As she got up to speak, the room became quiet.

"We must not give up hope. [. . .] Every one of us who loves you and has faith in you is working tirelessly [. . .] to shut the camp down so you can work, move around, and live as free human beings again, and to get you into the country legally under the quotas. That day, [when you arrived] at the Statue of Liberty, you told me the air of America smells like free air. Believe me; we want you to breathe it."

\*\*\*

On Saturday, December 22, Ruth was working at her desk in Washington when she heard an announcement on the radio. President Truman would make a statement this evening on immigration and refugees.

## *President Truman*

Harry S. Truman was the thirty-third president of the United States. He was Franklin D. Roosevelt's vice president and succeeded him when President Roosevelt died in April 1945. Truman served as president until 1953. He was the first world leader to recognize the State of Israel.

That evening, Ruth sat in her favorite armchair and listened as President Truman announced that the Oswego refugees would be allowed to remain in the United States. He hadn't finished speaking when her phone rang. It was Manya, calling from Oswego.

"We're staying!" Manya sobbed. "The camp has gone wild. Everyone is hugging and kissing and crying. Ruthie, are you there? Do you hear me?"

Ruth nodded but couldn't speak. Her voice was too choked with tears.

# Author's Note

I've ended this book with the story of the Oswego refugees, but that is only the beginning of Ruth Gruber's incredible career. In 1947, she went to Jerusalem for the *New York Herald Tribune* to cover the United Nations Special Committee on Palestine (UNSCOP) while it debated establishing a Jewish State. There, she heard about the *Exodus 1947*, a refugee ship carrying 4,500 Holocaust survivors. Her coverage of that story brought world attention to their plight. In 1948, Ruth returned to Israel to write about Israel's war of independence. In 1949, she participated in Operation Magic Carpet, a mission to bring Jewish refugees from Yemen to Israel.

Throughout her life, Ruth valued family. She met her husband, Phillip, in 1951. Their daughter, Celia, was born in 1952, followed by their son, David, in 1954. Ruth could finally use the cradle that Marfa, the Yakut woman, had given her. Once she had a family, Ruth spent most of her time at home in Manhattan, writing whenever she could.

Ruth Gruber takes a photo while working in Alaska in 1941.

Phillip was a hands-on father who looked after the children when Ruth went on short trips. But when Ruth took longer trips—as in the summer of 1963, when she received a grant to study immigrant experiences in Israel—the family went with her.

Phillip died in 1968, and in 1974 Ruth married Henry Rosen, a social activist. Her second marriage gave her three stepdaughters: Barbara Seaman, who died in 2008; Jeri Drucker; and Elaine Rosner-Jeria. Ruth had nine grandchildren and six great-grandchildren.

Ruth Gruber (*third row, third from left*) stands with Jewish refugees from Europe in 1946, shortly after the end of World War II. Ruth worked passionately to support war refugees, including the people she brought to the United States aboard the *Henry Gibbons* in 1944.

In 1987, at the age of seventy-six, Ruth traveled to remote mountain villages in Ethiopia to record the stories of Ethiopian Jews. This project became her book *Rescue: The Exodus of the Ethiopian Jews*. Twenty years later, at the age of ninety-five, in her book *Witness*, Ruth wrote, "There are now more than 100,000 Ethiopian Jews living in Israel. They became part of that Jewish community made up of an ingathering from all over the world."

In 2001, at age ninety, Ruth completed a twenty-city tour to publicize four of her books that were being reprinted. When people asked her for the secret to her success, she said, "Have dreams, have visions, and let no obstacle stop you."

And she didn't. Speaking to an audience at Stony Brook University in Stony Brook, New York, in 2008—at age ninety-seven—she explained her motivation for the work she had done.

"Whenever I saw that Jews were in danger," she said, "I covered that story."

Ruth Gruber died on November 17, 2016, at the age of 105. During her seventy-year career, she wrote nineteen books. She won many awards, both for her writing and her humanitarian work. Her life inspired two films: the documentary *Ahead of Time* (2010), which covers her life from her childhood in Brooklyn through the *Exodus* story; and the made-for-TV movie *Haven* (2001), which is about the Oswego refugees.

"My mother was cool," Ruth's daughter, Celia, told me. "She was generous and helpful, and passionate about her work." One of Celia's favorite memories is when the movie *Haven* was shot in Toronto in 2001. Celia and Ruth were extras in the film.

"We played refugees," Celia said. "Natasha Richardson played Ruth. Natasha and my mother became good friends."

Celia describes her mother as short in stature but formidable in personality and drive. "My mother loved fashion. She had many knitted outfits designed by Pnina Shalom, an Israeli designer. Mother's favorite color was turquoise, and she loved big necklines and chunky jewelry. She was a very elegant lady."

I want to thank Celia for sharing her memories with me. Although I never got to meet Ruth, I am honored to have had the opportunity to write about her extraordinary life.

# Glossary

**Antisemitism:** a form of racism based on hatred of and prejudice against Jews

**Ashkenazi:** Eastern and Central European Jews and their descendants

**bush pilot:** a pilot flying in rough terrain with no prepared landing strips or runways

**capitalism:** an economic and political system in which trade and industry are controlled by private owners for profit

**Catholic:** a member of a branch of Christianity

**chuppah:** a canopy that the bride and groom stand under during the wedding ceremony

**communism:** a political system in which all property is owned by the State and people are paid according to their needs

**dissertation:** a long essay on a particular subject, especially one written for a doctor of philosophy (PhD) degree

**fascism:** a form of far-right, authoritarian government characterized by dictatorial power, forcible suppression of opposition, as well as strong regimentation of society and of the economy. Fascism developed in the early twentieth century in Europe.

**fellowship:** a prize or a temporary paid position

**gulag:** the network of forced labor camps in the Soviet Union

**Indigenous:** native to a particular place

**Kiddush:** a blessing over wine

**Nazi Party:** the National Socialist German Workers' Party, led by Adolf Hitler in Germany. The party believed in racist policies, military leadership, nationalism, and antisemitic policies.

**PhD:** the highest degree awarded by a graduate school in a field of academic study

**pogrom:** an organized attack on a particular group, such as the Jews

**Protestant:** a member of a branch of Christianity that is separate from Catholicism

**quota:** a minimum or maximum number, such as the number of a particular group of people allowed to do something

**Shabbos:** the Jewish Sabbath

**shtetl:** a small Jewish village or town in Eastern Europe or Russia

**shul:** a synagogue

**Soviet Union:** the name given to the Russian Empire after the 1917 revolution, short for the Union of Soviet Socialist Republics (USSR)

**Siberia:** a vast territory in northern Asia that is a major part of Russia

**swastika:** an ancient symbol that was adopted by Hitler and his followers and turned into an emblem of the Nazi Party

**thesis:** a long essay involving original research, written by a candidate for a master's or PhD degree

**Yiddish:** the traditional language of Eastern European Jews. Yiddish is based on German, Hebrew, and several other languages including Polish and Russian

# Source Notes

6    Robert D. McFadden, "Ruth Gruber, a Fearless Chronicler of the Jewish Struggle, Dies at 105." *New York Times*, November 17, 2016. https://www.nytimes.com/2016/11/18/nyregion/ruth-gruber-dead.html?_r=0

11    Ruth Gruber, *Ahead of Time: My Early Years as a Foreign Correspondent*, 20

12    Ibid., 19

14    Ibid., 31

16    Ibid., 32

16    Ibid., 34

18    Ibid., 66

19    Ibid., 72

19–20    Ibid., 73

20    Ibid., 74–77

22    Ibid., 83

25    Ibid., 102

26–27    Ibid., 102

27–28    Ibid., 111–112

30    Ibid., 118

31    Ibid., 120

33    Ibid., 135–136

37    Ibid., 159

39–40    Ibid., 165

41–45    Ibid., 175–180

46–47    Ibid., 184

52    Ibid., 204–205

53    Ibid., 208

54    Ibid., 232

55    Ibid., 262

56–59    Ibid., 263–66

61–63    Ibid., 305–309

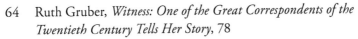

64     Ruth Gruber, *Witness: One of the Great Correspondents of the Twentieth Century Tells Her Story*, 78

64–65     Ibid., 79

71–72     Ibid., 66

73     Ibid., 68

74     Ruth Gruber, *Haven: The Dramatic Story of 1,000 World War II Refugees and How They Came to America*, 97

77–78     Ibid., 100–102

79     Ibid., 104

80     Ibid., 129

82     Ibid., 134

83     Ibid., 137

84–85     Ibid., 144

86     Ibid., 153

87     Ibid., 156

89–90     Ibid., 183–184

90     Emma Lazarus, "The New Colossus," National Park Service, www.nps.gov/stli/learn/historyculture/colossus.htm

91–93     *Haven*, 201

93     Ibid., 207

94–95     Ibid., 211–215

97     Ibid., 220

97–98     Ibid., 325–326

100     *Witness*, 70

103     Ibid., 72

104     *Haven*, 283

108     *Witness*, 404

108     Lynn Wexler, "Ruth Gruber, 20th Century Iconic Woman, Trailblazer and Award Winning Photojournalist." *David Magazine*, October 2017. https://davidlv.com/content/ruth-gruber

108     McFadden

108–109     Celia Michaels, interview with the author

# Timeline

**1911**   Ruth Gruber is born in New York City.

**1914**   World War I begins.

**1917**   The United States enters the war.

**1918**   World War I ends with the Allied powers (France, Great Britain, and the United States) defeating Germany.

**1924**   US government passes a quota on the immigration of Jews, Italians, Greeks, and people from Eastern Europe.

**1926**   Ruth enters New York University at the age of 15.

**1929**   Ruth gets her master's degree in German.

**1931–1932**   Ruth goes to Germany and gets her PhD.

She returns to New York and begins writing for newspapers.

**1933**   Adolf Hitler is elected chancellor of Germany.

The German government starts passing anti-Jewish laws.

**1935**   Ruth returns to Germany.

She also visits Russia and becomes the first foreign journalist to visit the Soviet Arctic.

**1939**   Germany invades Poland on September 1. World War II begins.

Ruth's book *I Went to the Soviet Arctic* is released.

**1941**   Secretary of the Interior Harold Ickes hires Ruth and sends her to Alaska, where she would work until 1943.

On December 7, 1941, Japan attacks the US naval base at Pearl Harbor. The United States enters the war.

**1944**   Ruth brings 982 refugees to the United States and stays with them in the Oswego refugee camp.

**1945** President Franklin D. Roosevelt dies. Harry S. Truman becomes president.

World War II ends.

President Truman allows the Oswego refugees to remain in the United States.

**1947** Ruth is in Jerusalem covering the United Nations hearings on Palestine when she hears about the refugees aboard the ship *Exodus 1947*. Her coverage calls worldwide attention to the plight of Holocaust survivors.

The United Nations vote in favor of establishing the State of Israel.

**1948** The State of Israel forms.

Ruth covers the Israeli War of Independence for the *New York Herald Tribune*.

Her book *Destination Palestine: The Story of the Haganah Ship Exodus 1947* is released.

**1949** Ruth goes to Yemen to report on Operation Magic Carpet, the rescue of Yemeni Jews.

**1983** Ruth's book *Haven: The Dramatic Story of 1000 World War II Refugees and How They Came to America* is published.

**1987** Ruth covers Operation Moses, the Israeli government's rescue of Ethiopian Jews.

**2016** Ruth Gruber dies at the age of 105.

# Selected Bibliography

Gruber, Ruth. *Ahead of Time: My Early Years as a Foreign Correspondent.* New York: Wynwood Press, 1991.

———. *Haven: The Dramatic Story of 1,000 World War II Refugees and How They Came to America.* New York: Open Road Integrated Media, 2014.

———. *Witness: One of the Great Correspondents of the Twentieth Century Tells Her Story.* New York: Schocken Books, 2007.

# Index

## About the Author

Rona Arato is a former teacher and an award-winning author of more than 20 children's books. Many of her books deal with human rights, tackling antisemitism and its effects on the Jewish community. She is a frequent presenter at schools and community organizations.

## About the Illustrator

Isabel Muñoz is an artist and a children's book illustrator. She works from a tiny, colorful studio in the north of Spain.